My Best Preschool Workbook Toddler Coloring Book

A Fun Coloring Book With Shapes, Lines, Objects & Animals. Big Activity Workbook for Preschoolers, Toddlers & Kids
(Vol. 1)

By
Thrive Creative Kids

HAVE A QUESTION OR FEEDBACK? LET US KNOW!

EMAIL: info@thrivecoloringbooks.com

WEBSITE: ThriveColoringBooks.com

THIS BOOK BELONGS TO:

____

____

____

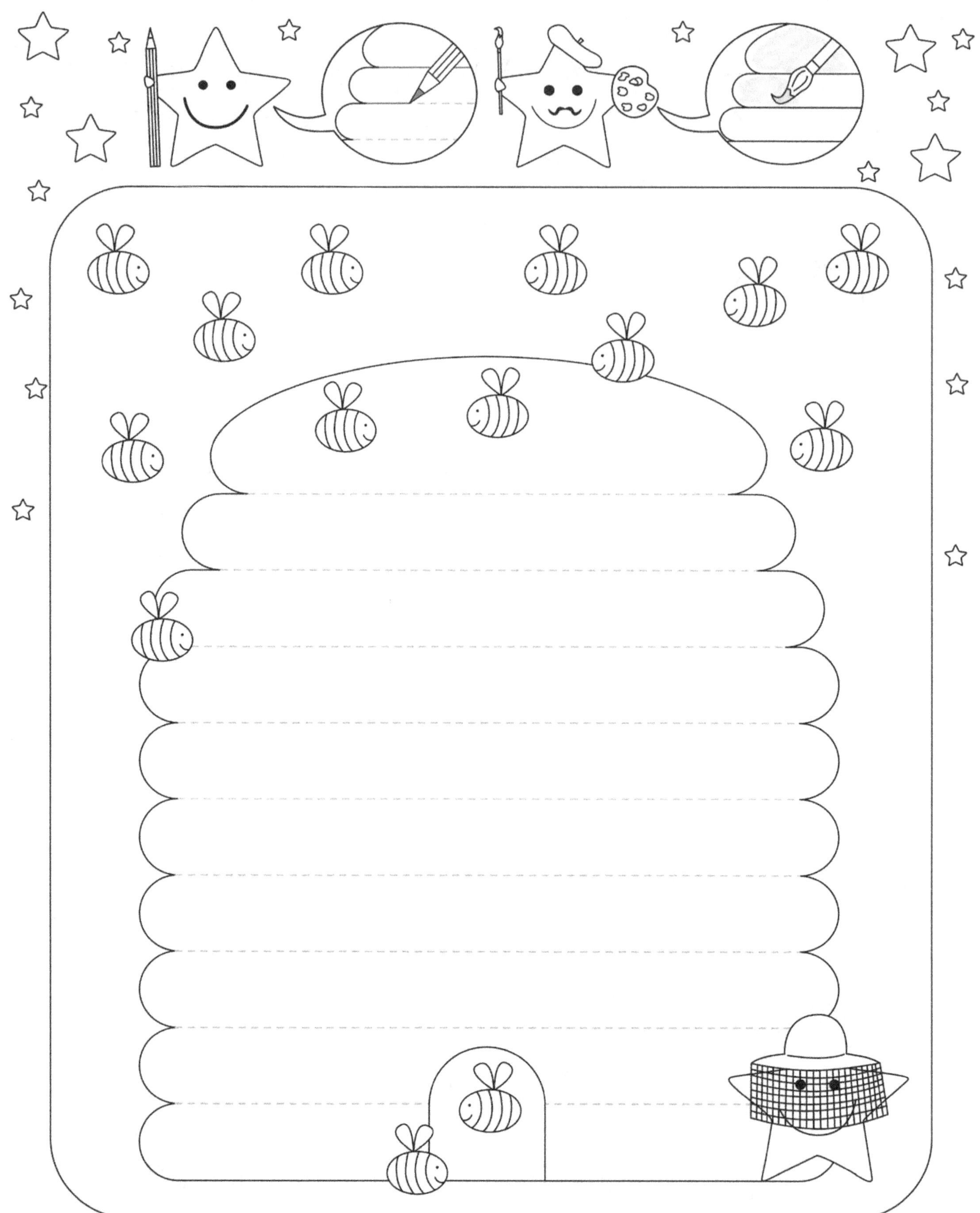

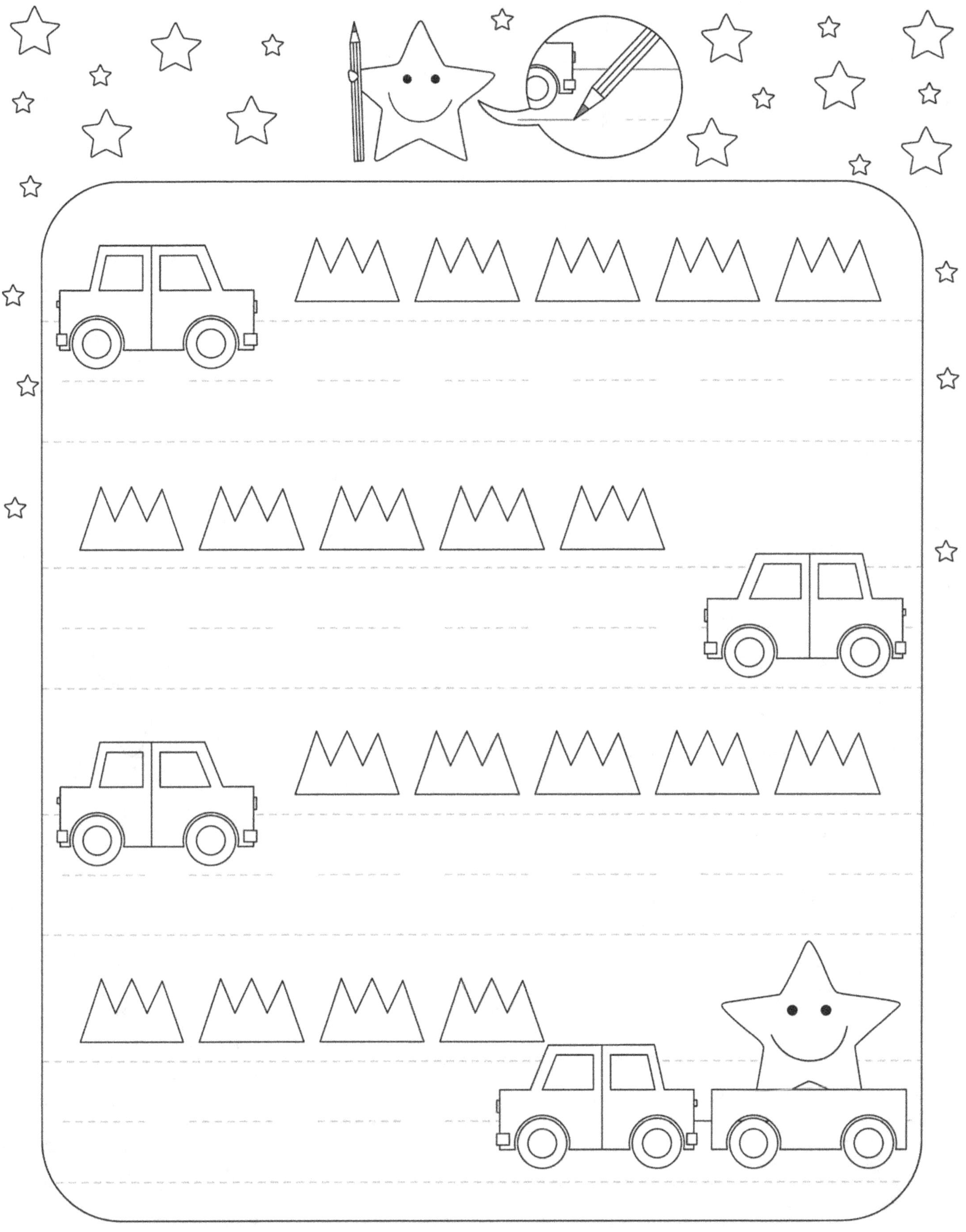

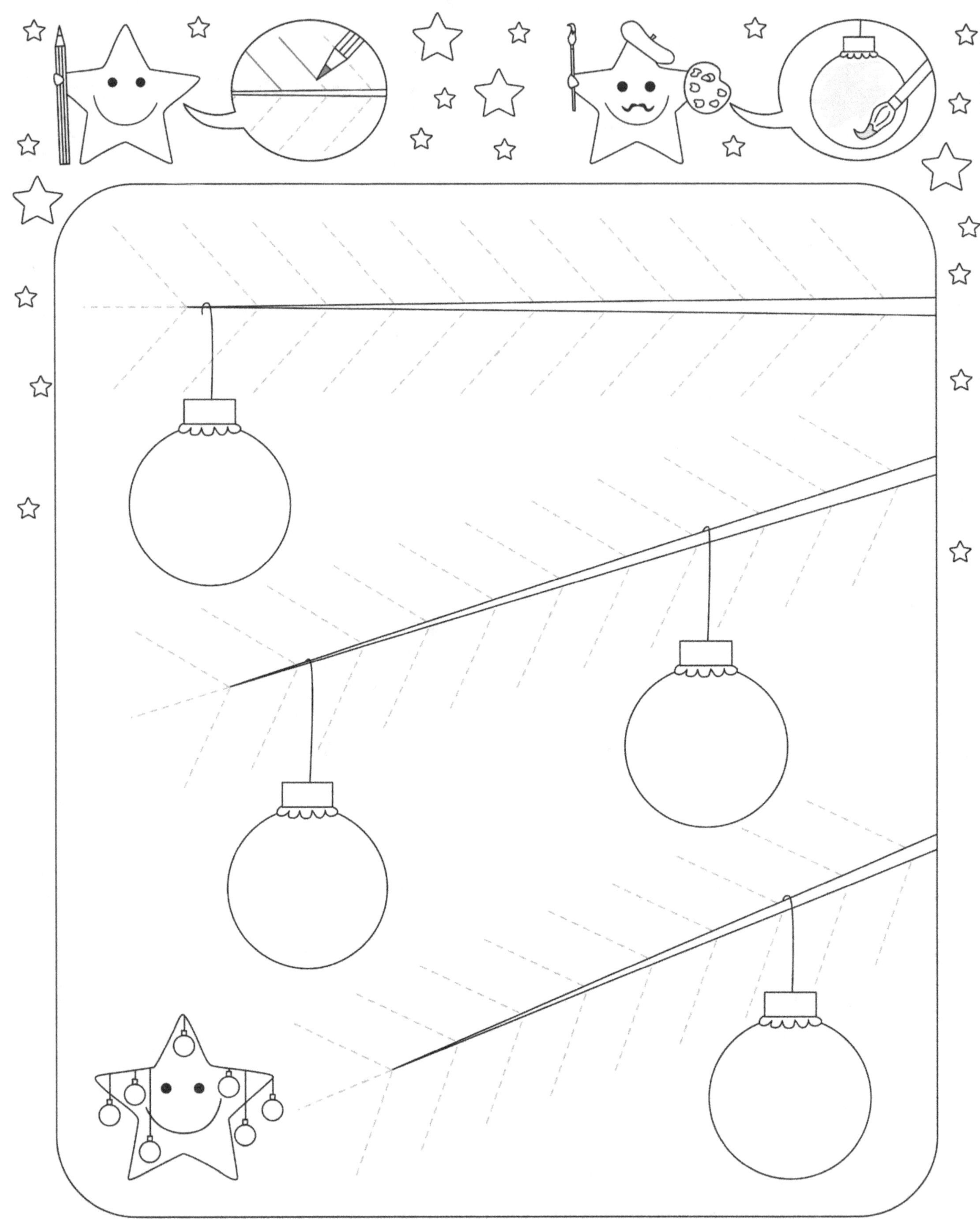

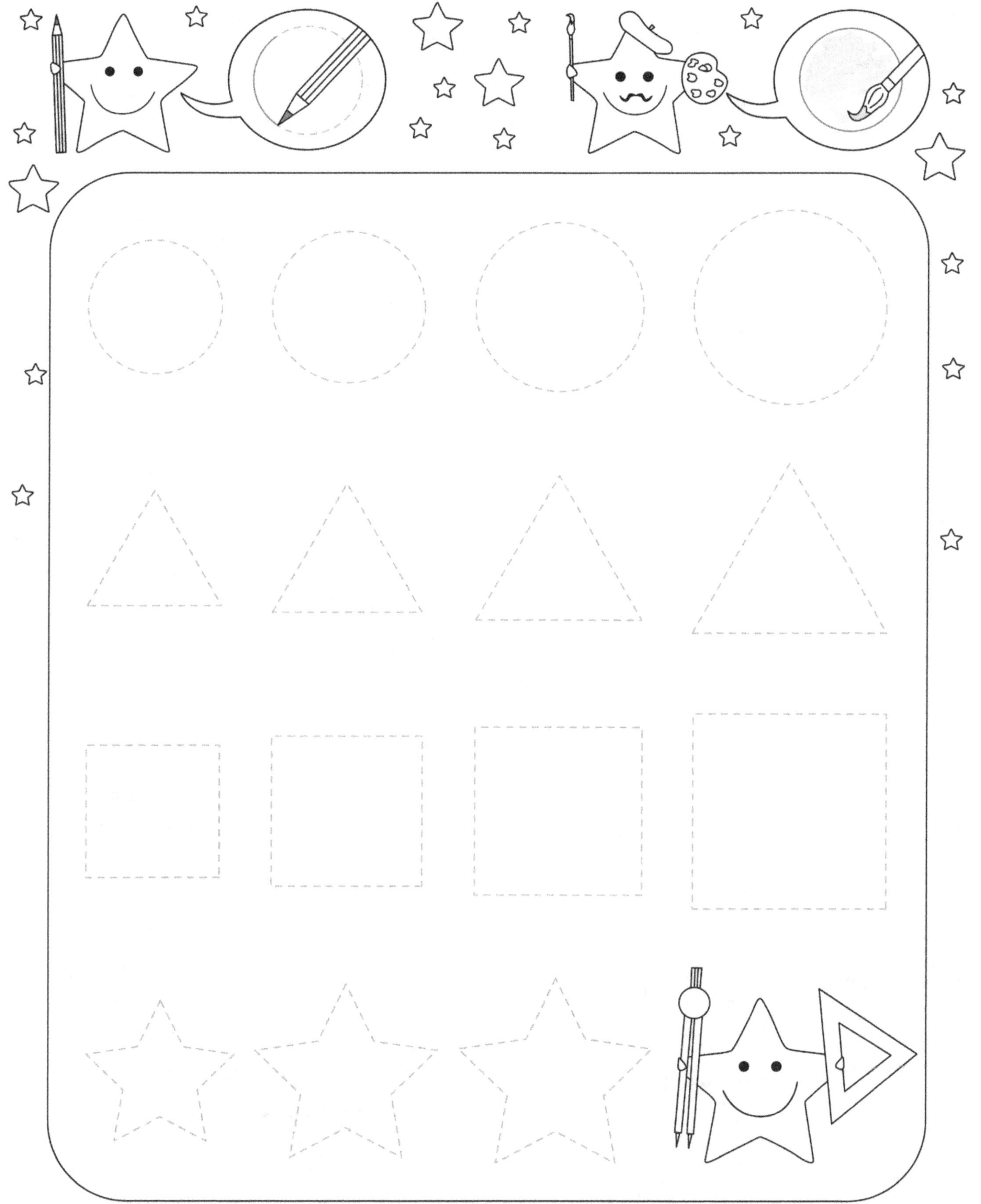

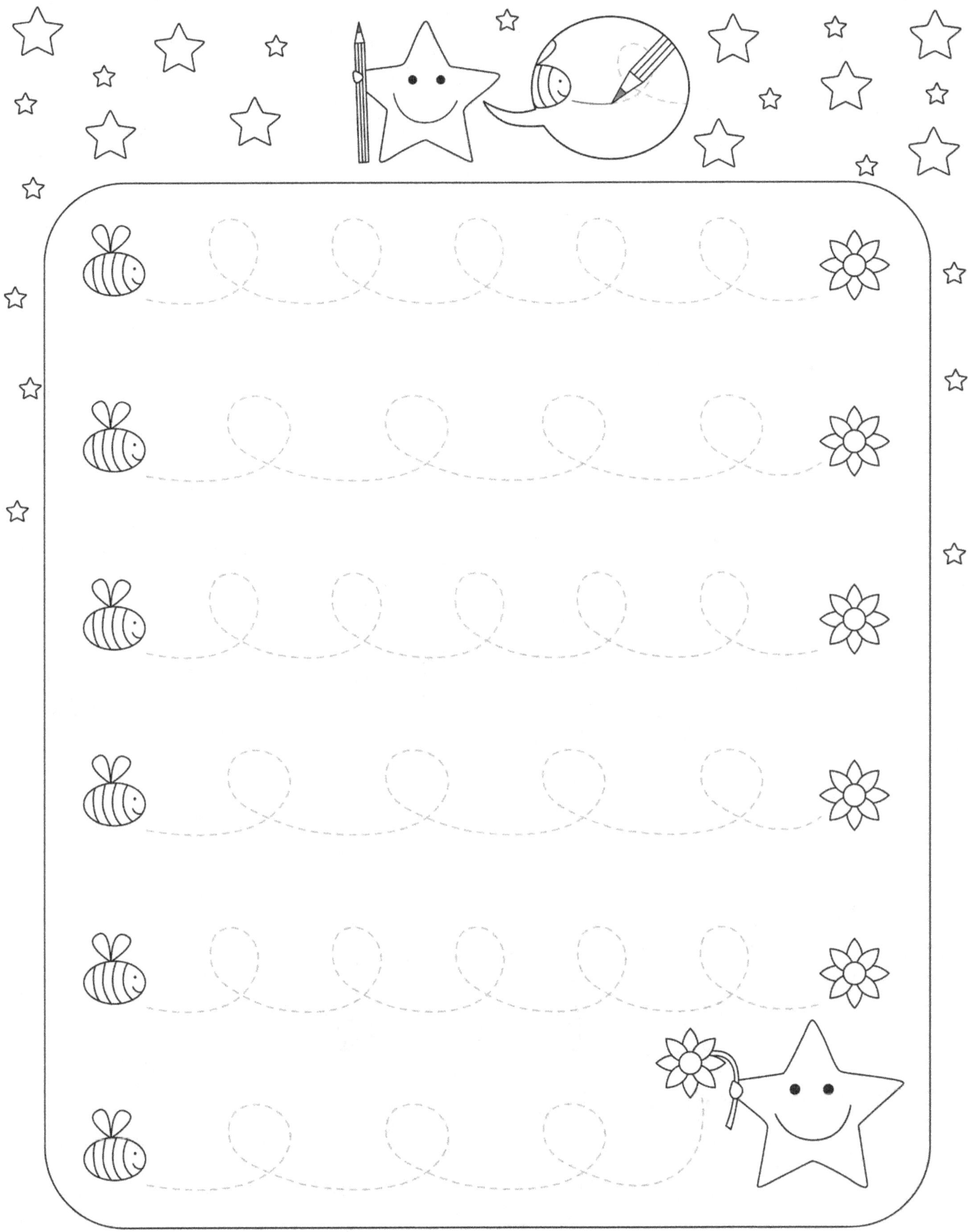

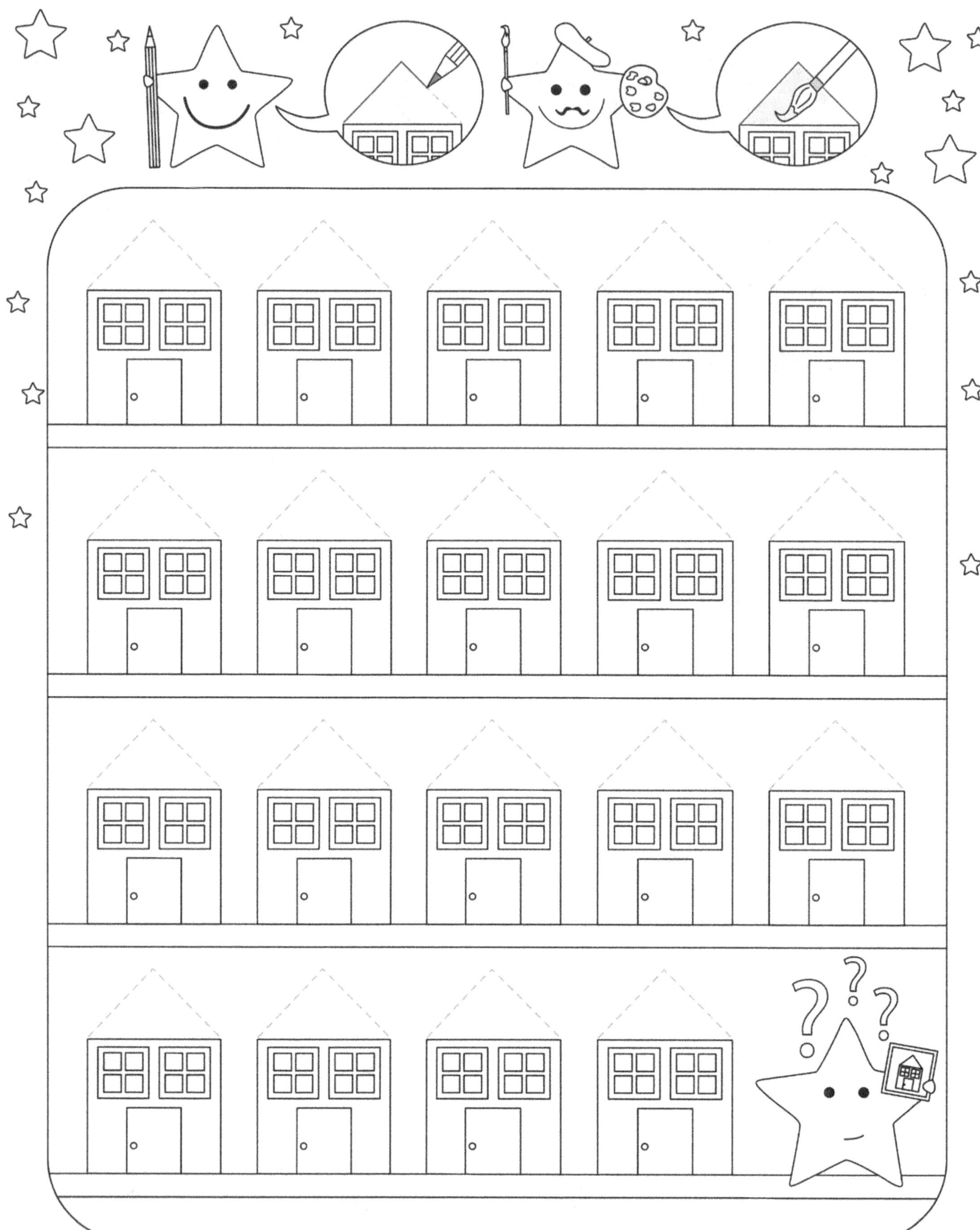

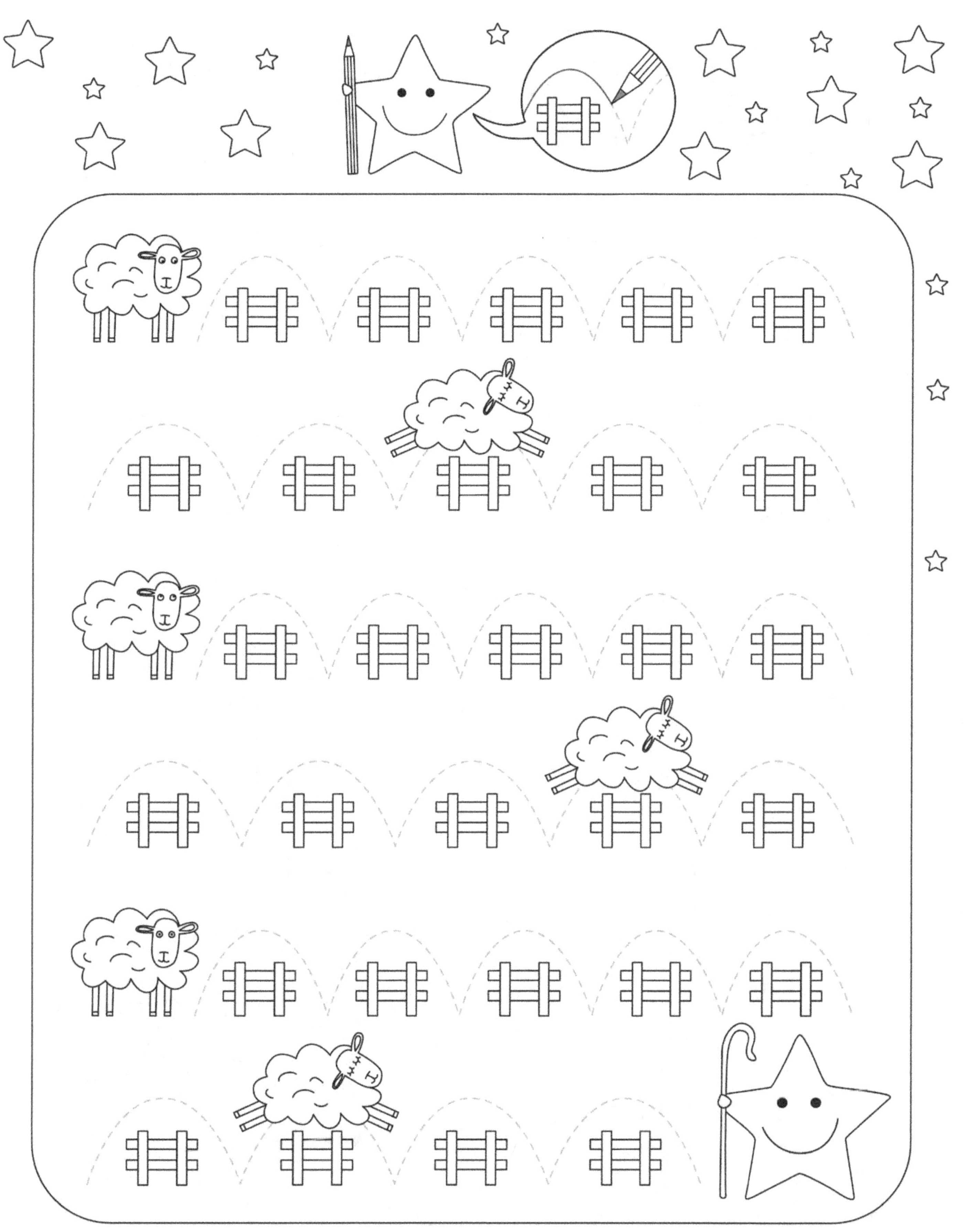

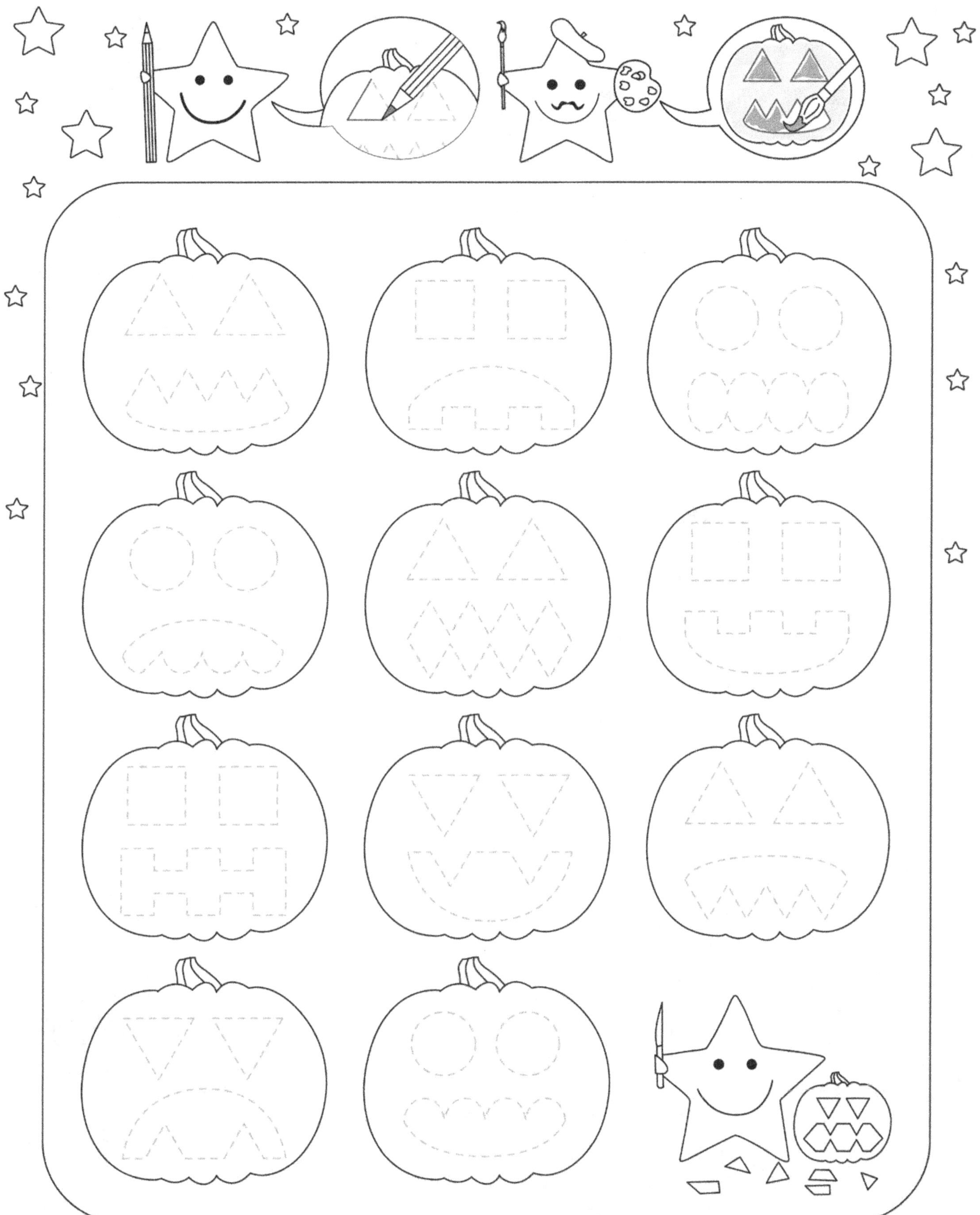

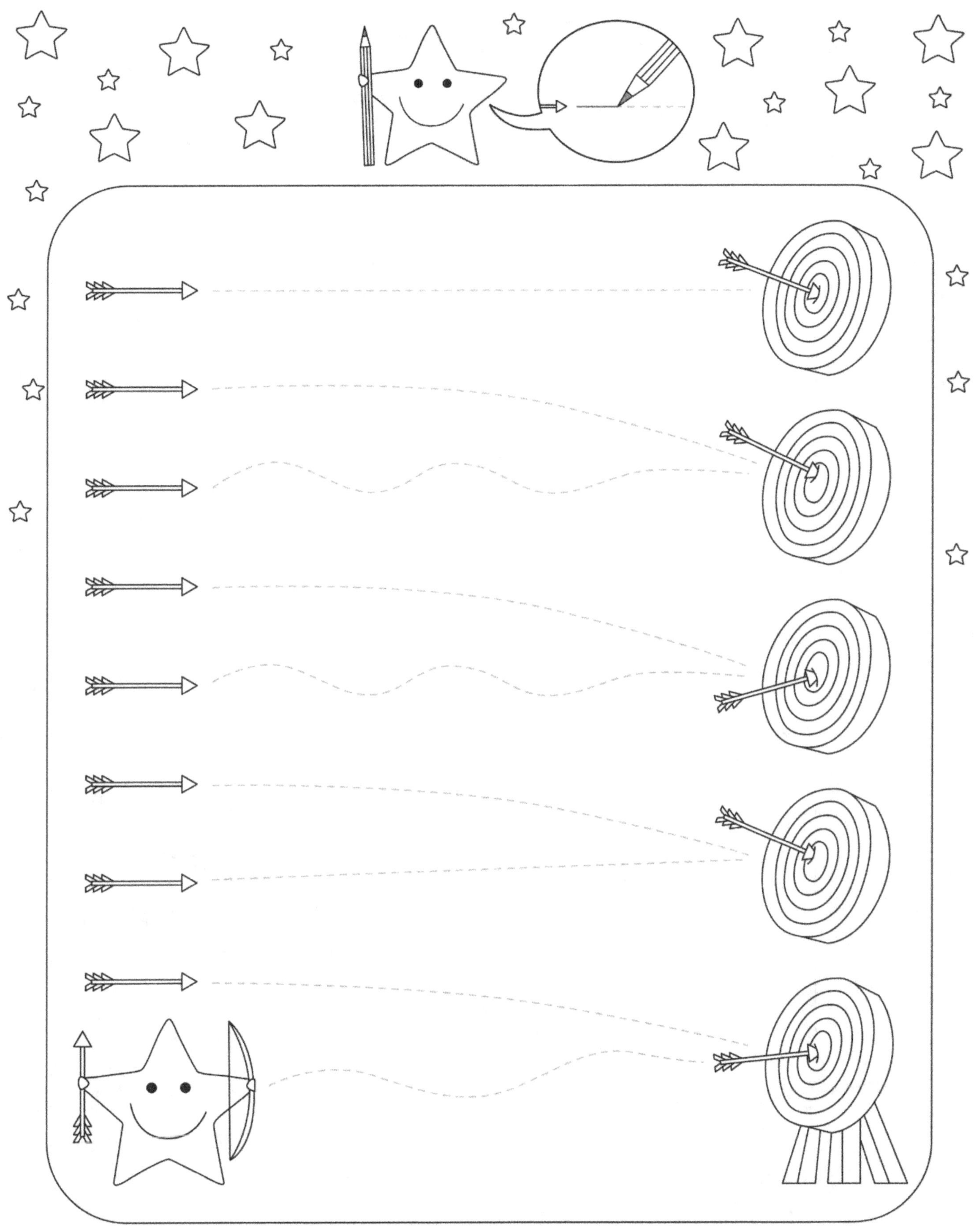

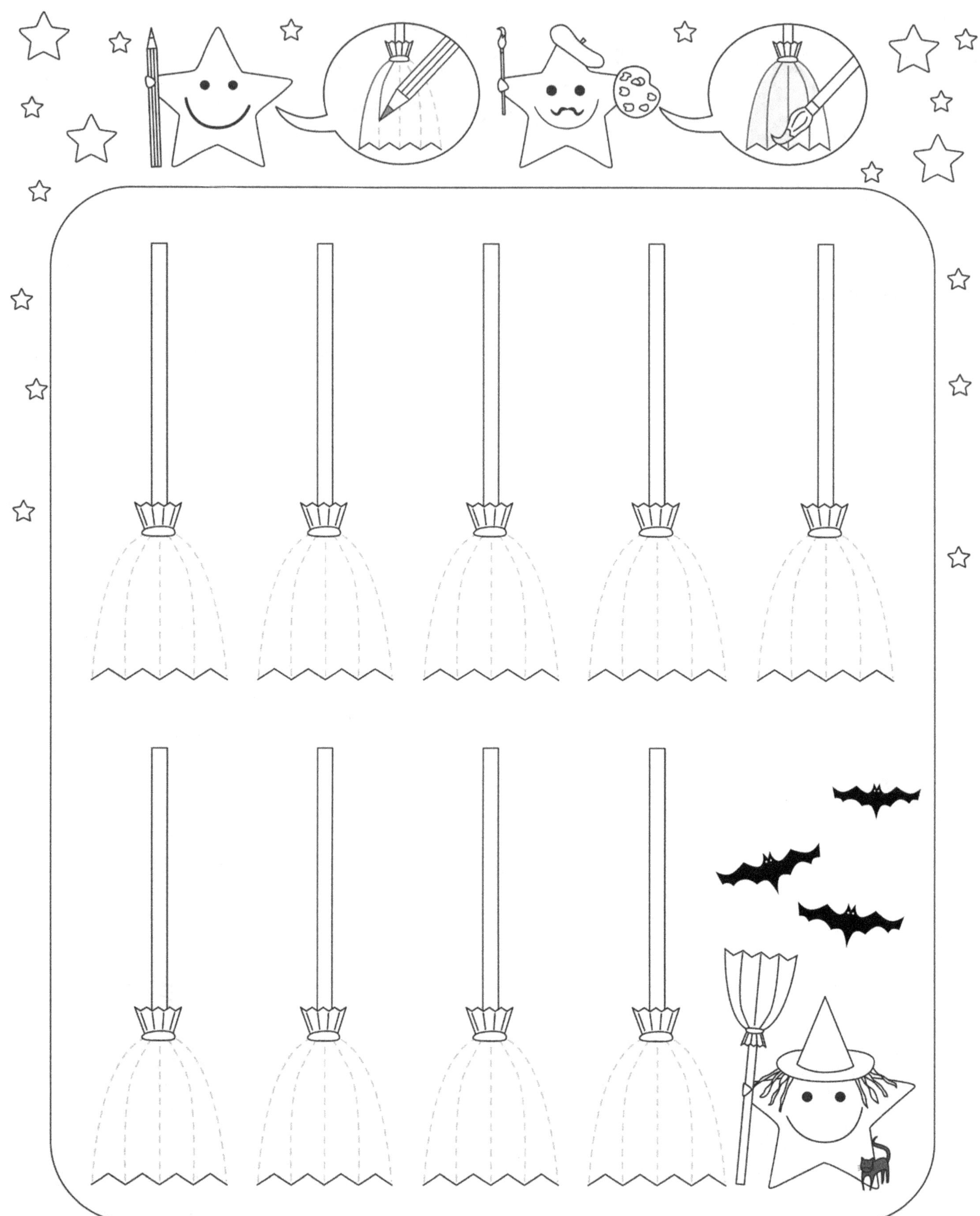

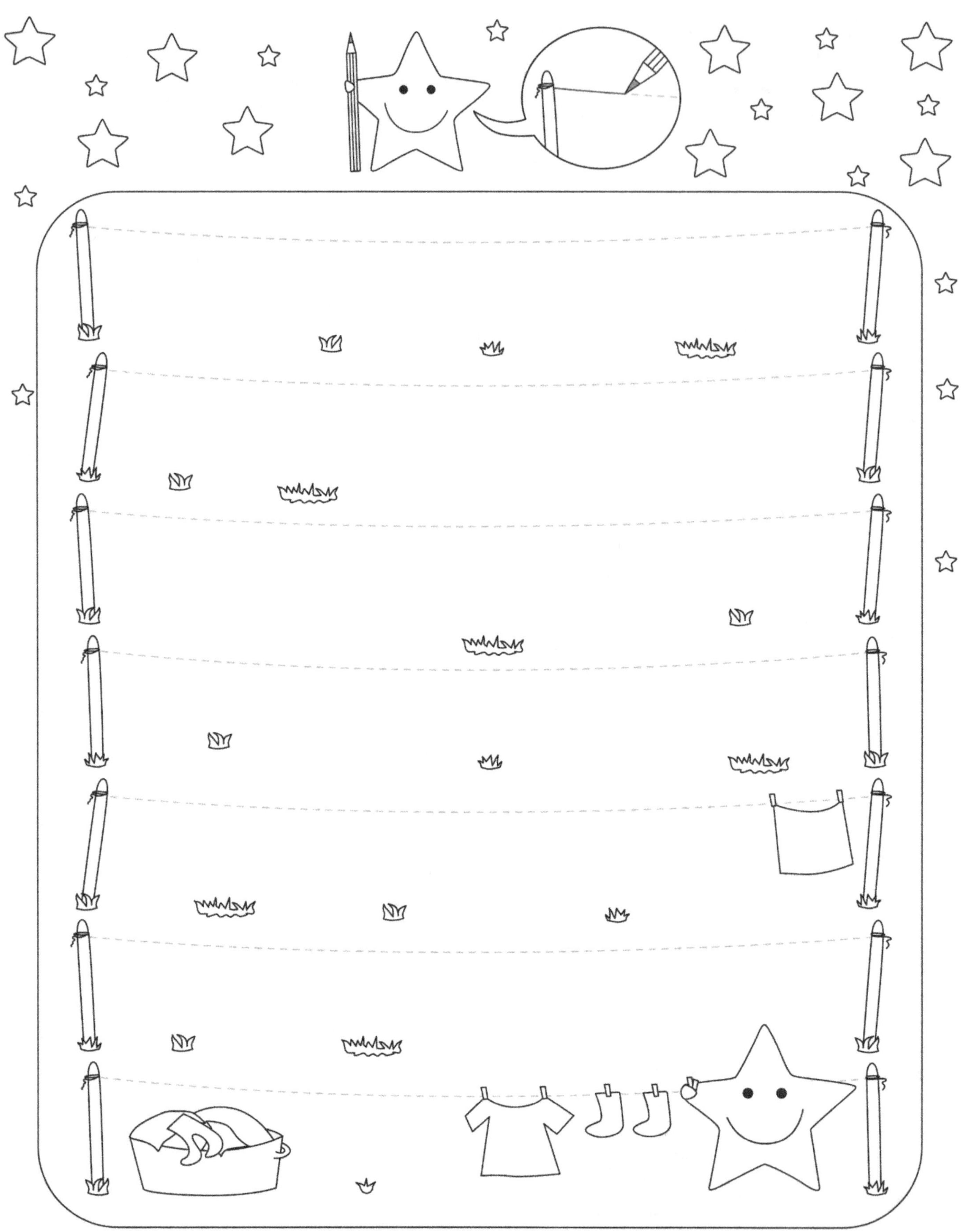

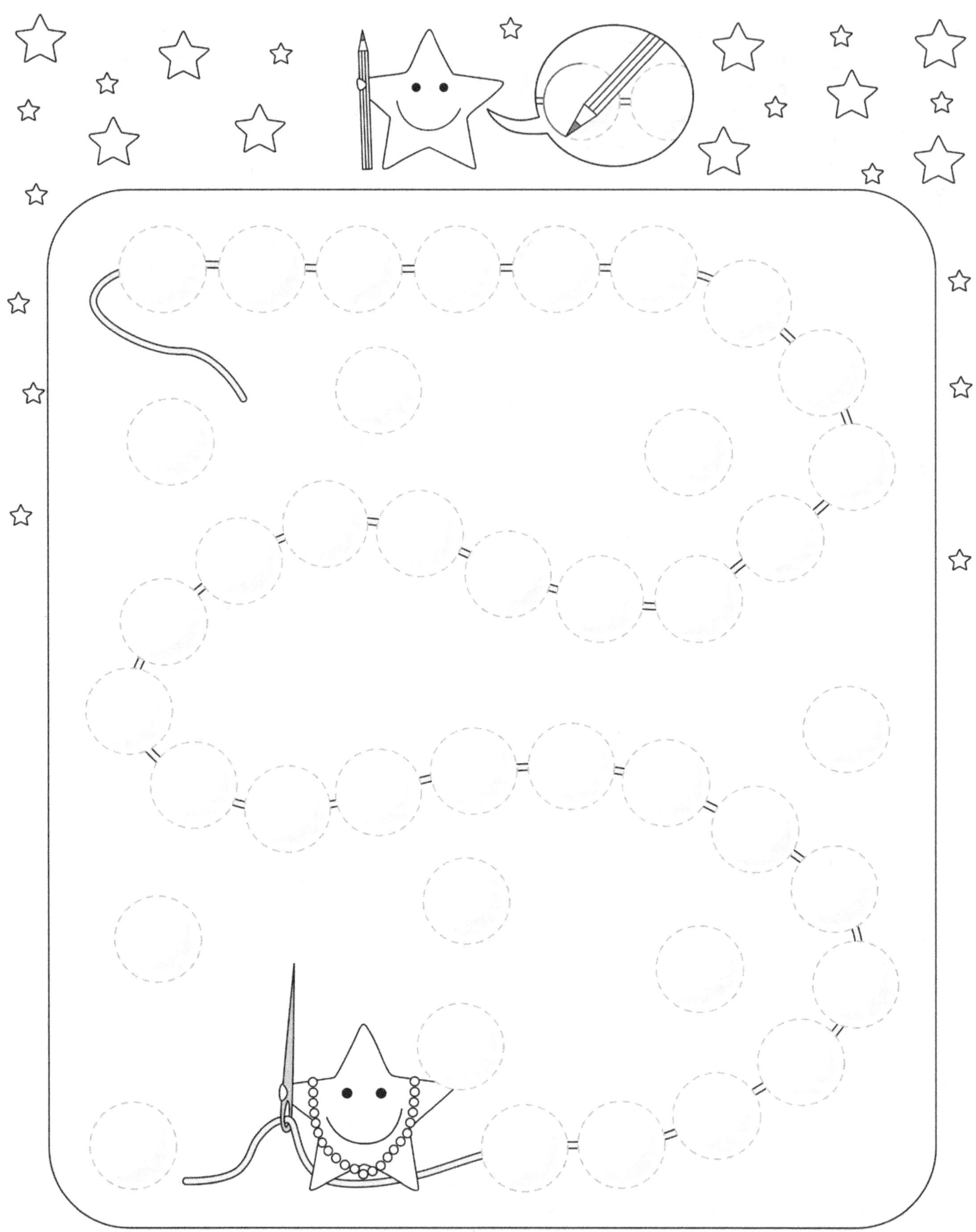

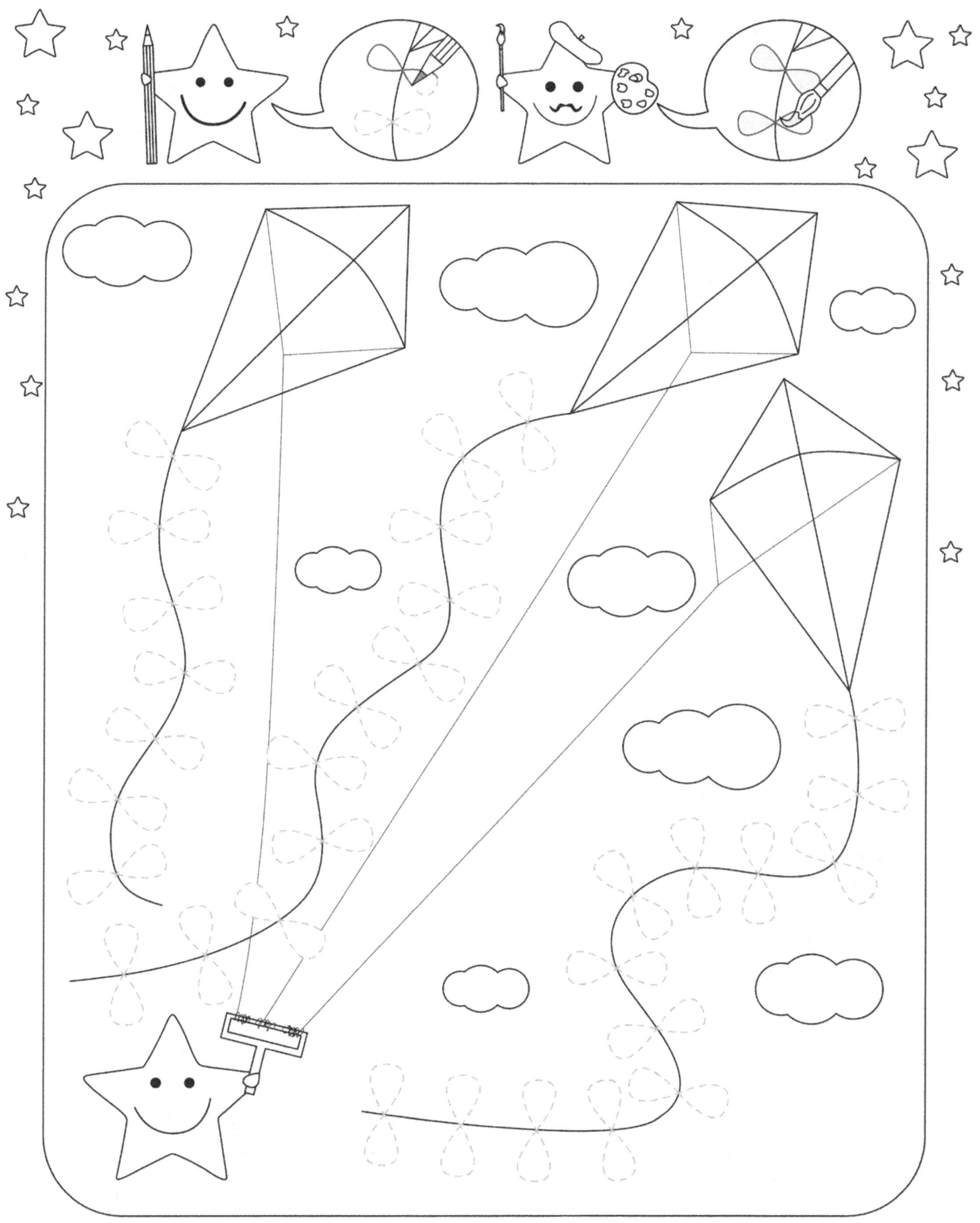

DID YOUR CHILD ENJOYED COLORING THIS PRESCHOOL WORKBOOK?

IF YES, THEN SHARE THE LOVE WITH YOUR FRIENDS AND FAMILIES OR GIFT THEM ONE AND LET THEIR KIDS ALSO CONTINUE THE FUN

IF YOUR KID ENJOYED COLORING THIS BOOK, TAKE A PICTURE OF THEIR LOVELY COLORING PAGE AND SHARE IT TO THE WORLD ON AMAZON

KINDLY TYPE THE LINK BELOW INTO YOUR WEB BROWSER & WRITE A FEEDBACK ON AMAZON

GET IN TOUCH WITH US

JOIN THE THRIVE COLORING BOOK ONLINE COMMUNITY

EMAIL: info@thrivecoloringbooks.com

WEBSITE: www.thrivecoloringbooks.com

FACEBOK PAGE: @thrivecoloringbooks

PINTEREST: @thrivecoloringbooks

AMAZON: Amazon.com/author/thrivecreativekids

www.ingramcontent.com/pod-product-compliance
Lightning Source LLC
Chambersburg PA
CBHW081319250726
48662CB00008B/2651